MW01094697

PARTNERING WITH

CREATIVE EXPRESSION

PROPHETIC GATES

YVONNE MARTINEZ

PROPHETIC GATES

Copyright © 2010 by Yvonne Martinez
All rights reserved

This book is protected by the copyright law of the United States of America. This book may not be copied or reprinted for commercial gain or profit. The use of short quotations or occasional page copying for personal or group study is permitted and encouraged. Permission will be granted upon request.

Unless otherwise noted, all Scripture quotations are from the Holy Bible,
New International Version. Copyright © 1973, 1978, 1984, International Bible Society. Used by permission of Zondervan. All rights reserved.

The "NIV" and "New International Version" trademarks are registered in the United States Patent and Trademark Office by International Bible Society.
Use of either trademark requires the permission of International Bible Society.

ISBN 1449549306

EAN-13 9781449549305

Printed in the United States of America

Published and distributed by Stillwater Lavender
www.StillwaterLavender.com

DEDICATED
TO MY DAUGHTER
NOEL,
YOU ARE AMAZING,
TALENTED,
PROPHETIC
AND BEAUTIFUL.
THE GATES OF HEAVEN
AWAIT YOUR INVASION!

YVONNE MARTINEZ
IS THE AUTHOR OF
**DANCING ON THE GRAVES
OF YOUR PAST**
(BOOK AND WORKBOOK)
AND
**PRAYERS OF
PROPHETIC DECLARATION**

AVAILABLE AT:

WWW.STILLWATERLAVENDER.COM

MY THANKS TO ALL THE PASTORS AND STAFF UNDER BILL JOHNSON, BETHEL CHURCH IN REDDING, CA, FOR ALL YOU DO TO ADVANCE REVIVAL AND KINGDOM CULTURE.

RECOMMENDED READING

When Heaven Invades Earth
Bill Johnson, (Destiny Image)

Basic Training for the Prophetic Ministry
Kris Vallotton, (Destiny Image)

You All May Prophesy!
Steve Thompson, (Morning Star Publications)

The Happy Intercessor
Beni Johnson, (Destiny Image)

The Ultimate Treasure Hunt
Kevin Dedmon, (Destiny Image)

Culture of Honor
Danny Silk, (Destiny Image)

BETHEL CHURCH

www.ibethel.org

PROPHETIC GATES

TABLE OF CONTENTS

WHAT ARE YOU SENSING, SEEING, FEELING, OR HEARING FROM HIM?

_____

_____

_____

_____

_____

_____

_____

_____

_____

_____

_____

_____

_____

_____

CHAPTER 1

GATES OF
PROPHETIC CULTURE

Jesus opened the gates to prophetic and supernatural activity so every Christian can hear from God. God is talking to His church and He is talking to His people. Our increased awareness is an invitation to listen and partner with what God is saying both *to* us and *through* us. Let's embrace our inheritance in the Kingdom and partner with all God has for us.

It is time to enter your prophetic destiny...

WHAT ARE YOU SENSING, SEEING, FEELING, OR HEARING FROM HIM?

_____

_____

_____

_____

_____

_____

_____

_____

_____

_____

_____

_____

_____

_____

_____

_____

_____

The source of true prophecy doesn't come from the human spirit or mind, rather through a supernatural gift from God. Prophecy is receiving Divine supernatural insight on behalf of someone to whom God wants to reveal His love, presence, and power. Paul gives us a simple definition of prophetic ministry in 1 Corinthians 14:3 where he tells us, *"But everyone who prophesies speaks to men for their strengthening, encouragement and comfort."*

Three of the nine prophetic gifts outlined in 1 Corinthians 12:8-10 are a *word of knowledge, a word of wisdom, and discerning of spirits.* These three gifts are revelatory in nature. They reveal information previously only known by God. Prophecy is the communication of God's revelatory word.

When we keep to the basic purpose Paul describes in 1 Corinthians 14:3 we are able to hear from God and speak to others in such a way as to impact their lives for the better. Revelation that strengthens, encourages, and comforts, reveals the truth that God is in a good mood and He has good things to say bringing hope in the face of turmoil and faith on the heels of disappointment.

Prophecy was not meant to be confined within the walls of a church building. When the prophetic gifts move outside church walls it brings an unsaved generation into connection with a loving and caring

WHAT ARE YOU SENSING, SEEING, FEELING, OR HEARING FROM HIM?

_____

_____

_____

_____

_____

_____

_____

_____

_____

_____

_____

_____

_____

_____

_____

_____

_____

God. Communication of revelatory prophetic words can be through many different vehicles or methods. Using gift of prophecy to strengthen, encourage and comfort calls out the treasure in people and moves them closer to their destiny.

In I Samuel 9:17 – 10:9, the story about Samuel and Saul is a great example. Saul is looking for lost donkeys and runs into Samuel, who has already received a prophetic word of knowledge from God about Saul's destiny.

As Samuel begins to talk to Saul, Saul discloses his low self esteem. Saul answered, *"But am I not a Benjamite, from the smallest tribe of Israel, and is not my clan the least of all the clans of the tribe of Benjamin? Why do you say such a thing to me?"*

Samuel encourages Saul to stay and visit with him so he can tell him *"all the things that are in his heart."* Samuel brings Saul to *"the high place"* and seats and serves him at the head of a table in the presence of invited guests. Samuel uses the time to build relationship with Samuel.

The next day Samuel, as promised, reveals the word of God to Saul, pouring a flask of oil on Saul's head and kissing him, saying, *"Has not the Lord anointed you leader over his inheritance?"*

Samuel used a variety of prophetic expressions to minister to Saul. Here are just a few examples:

WHAT ARE YOU SENSING, SEEING, FEELING, OR HEARING FROM HIM?

_____

_____

_____

_____

_____

_____

_____

_____

_____

_____

_____

_____

_____

_____

_____

_____

_____

- Samuel used words of encouragement through prophetic evangelism to open conversation into Saul's heart.

- Samuel used prophetic deliverance to discern and reach into Saul's heart to emotionally heal him from low self esteem.

- Samuel ministered to Saul's physical need to find the lost donkeys.

- Samuel did a prophetic act by taking Saul to the "high places," a place of significant spiritual authority and dominion.

- Samuel does another prophetic act showing favor to Saul and delights in him in the presence of others, further revealing and establishing Saul's prophetic destiny.

- Samuel used prophetic declaration to anoint Saul and call him into his destiny.

In 1 Samuel 10:9, the result of Saul's experiencing the prophetic word is revealed, "*As Saul turned to leave Samuel, God changed Saul's heart, and all these signs were fulfilled that day.*"

Samuel was a "seer." He had the position of a prophet and operated in the gift of prophecy. Samuel could "see" into Saul's heart and discern Saul was not walking toward his destiny. What if Saul said, " Hey

WHAT ARE YOU SENSING, SEEING, FEELING, OR HEARING FROM HIM?

_____

_____

_____

_____

_____

_____

_____

_____

_____

_____

_____

_____

_____

_____

_____

_____

Saul, I see you are a Benjemite and you are the smallest of your clan. I can see you think lowly of yourself and walk in fear you won't please your family if you don't find those lost donkeys. Samuel, you are going to be anointed as a King but later in life you are really going to make a mess of things. It doesn't look too good in the long run for you. But, I'll pray for you and hopefully God will turn things around."

Samuel didn't embarrass him. Samuel did not use his prophetic gift to call attention to, or declare, Saul's low self esteem or his fear. Rather, Samuel looked at Saul from God's perspective of what God desired him to become.

There are prophetic people who insist on speaking out the negative they see about people. It was the way they were trained and it is the way they feel they bring a *true* word of knowledge to someone. However, we already know *"all have sinned and fell short of the Glory of God"* (Romans 3:23). Sin *is* the falling short of God's Glory. The Cross forgives sin and releases His Glory is us. The true prophetic calls out treasure so those people who *"fell short of the Glory of God"* would respond with worship and declare the goodness of God.

In John 1:42, Jesus called Simon (which means broken reed) the name of *Peter* (which means rock.) Jesus prophetically declared and established that a broken reed would become a rock.

WHAT ARE YOU SENSING, SEEING, FEELING, OR HEARING FROM HIM?

_____

_____

_____

_____

_____

_____

_____

_____

_____

_____

_____

_____

_____

_____

_____

_____

Jesus called Peter into the rock he was destined to become. The prophetic calls a people into the Glory God has assigned to them. Prophetic revelation brings awareness to the destiny God allotted to them, thereby convicting them of their "falling short" and inviting them into right relationship with God.

In keeping with Paul's exhortation to strengthen (build up), encourage (to call near) and comfort (to cheer up), people will be blessed and the prophetic gift can never become a weapon of spiritual abuse.

My husband, Tony, and I attended a secular music festival where families are invited to enjoy a day of music and entertainment. Unfortunately, as the day progressed we noticed many parents purchased alcohol at the beer booth, progressively becoming intoxicated leaving their kids to run loose. This happened to be a group of people that my husband has built relationship with, so when we ask about sponsoring a booth with face painting, balloon animals, and personal portraits during the next year's festival they unanimously agreed.

We gathered a prophetically gifted team to help with ministry through out the day. Kids (and adults) anxiously lined up at our tables. As each one sat down to get their portrait sketched or face painted we had their undivided attention and an opportunity to seize that moment and speak into their lives.

WHAT ARE YOU SENSING, SEEING, FEELING, OR HEARING FROM HIM?

_____

_____

_____

_____

_____

_____

_____

_____

_____

_____

_____

_____

_____

_____

_____

_____

_____

We used the opportunity of "seeing" into their heart and in spite of what we "saw," we could flip that and call them out of their circumstance and into something better. One by one, we called out the treasures God showed us and their eyes would light up when we told them good things about their life. Everyone was hungry for someone to praise them and acknowledge their worth. We felt as though we were in the presence of future decision makers, scientists, architects, educators, politicians, perhaps even the leaders of nations. That's pretty cool! God's presence and power showed up during a secular music and alcohol fest and He allowed us to partner with Him and speak His heart into theirs.

As we opened conversations, more than a few voluntarily disclosed problems, broken family situations, or personal hardships. We had several opportunities to lead kids and parents to the Lord. Some of these people we continue in relationship with.

Prophetic gifts are available to every Christian. Paul, in I Corinthians 14:31 makes a declaration and also gives us invitation and permission to prophesy through his statement, "You all may prophesy." All Christians can hear from God and can learn how to turn their radio dial to His station. One of the reasons I wrote this book is to encourage people that prophetic gifts are diverse and expressive. We don't have to be stuck with the religious image of someone in the pulpit giving words of doom and gloom.

WHAT ARE YOU SENSING, SEEING, FEELING, OR HEARING FROM HIM?

_____

_____

_____

_____

_____

_____

_____

_____

_____

_____

_____

_____

_____

_____

_____

_____

_____

God isn't just equipping prophetic people; He is equipping a prophetic culture. Connecting with a prophetic community will heighten and maximize your prophetic anointing. You will find there is an increased impartation and grace when you operate under someone with a greater prophetic anointing than yours.

Continuing in 1Samuel:10 with the story of Samuel and Saul, Samuel gives Saul continued words of knowledge that culminate in Saul joining "*a procession of prophets coming down from the high place with lyres, tambourines, flutes and harps being played before them, and they will be prophesying.*" Samuel continues telling Saul, "*The Spirit of the Lord will come upon you in power, and you will prophesy with them; and you will be changed into a different person.*" As this part of the story concludes, Samuel tells Saul, "*Once these signs are fulfilled, do whatever your hand finds to do, for God is with you.*"

Samuel didn't give Saul something Saul didn't already have. The "different person" Saul became was the original man Saul was assigned to be. The great destiny was already in Saul awaiting activation.

A prophetic culture will activate the power of the Holy Spirit to change you into the person you are already destined to become. I am blessed to serve under and experience a unique combination of apostolic and prophetic covering.

WHAT ARE YOU SENSING, SEEING, FEELING, OR HEARING FROM HIM?

_____

_____

_____

_____

_____

_____

_____

_____

_____

_____

_____

_____

_____

_____

_____

_____

_____

_____

Bethel's leadership promotes a culture of honor that is taught by example and instruction. This framework of honor establishes leadership principles which promotes and nurtures a safe, healthy prophetic community. Those who rest under Bethel's umbrella find the operation of their supernatural and prophetic gifting is activated, elevated, and enriched.

Prophetic cultures are necessary to sustain and grow revelatory, supernatural gifts. A prophetic culture that establishes a system of honor and respect allows freedom and trust, accountability and growth, as well as diversity of expression.

How would you determine if you are in a prophetic community? First of all you would not be a lone ranger operating without accountability or absence of continued relationship. Second, you wouldn't be on display or a loose spiritual cannon, blasting people with correction and reading their personal mail in public.

Authentic relationship requires honor. Honor protects and covers. It doesn't embarrass or humiliate. Honor allows mercy to triumph over judgment. Honor and relationship are keys to spiritual growth.

Cultural elements:

- **Shared attitudes** - *A group of people whose practices identify the particular place, class, or time to which they belong.*

WHAT ARE YOU SENSING, SEEING, FEELING, OR HEARING FROM HIM?

_____

_____

_____

_____

_____

_____

_____

_____

_____

_____

_____

_____

_____

_____

_____

_____

- **Shared knowledge** – *The awareness and sophistication acquired through education and exposure.*

- **Shared purpose** - *The development of a skill or expertise through training or education in a particular system of thought or doctrine.*

- **Shared practices** - *The beliefs, customs, practices, and social behavior of a particular nation or people group.*

- **Shared growth** - *To nurture somebody or something, especially in order to advance their understanding or expertise.*

It is within the arrangement of an honoring, prophetic culture that I encourage and promote entering *Prophetic Gates* with diversity and expression.

WHAT ARE YOU SENSING, SEEING, FEELING, OR HEARING FROM HIM?

_____

_____

_____

_____

_____

_____

_____

_____

_____

_____

_____

_____

_____

_____

_____

_____

CHAPTER 2

GATES OF
PROPHETIC CREATIVITY

God creates. It isn't just what He does; it is who He *is*. Col. 1:16 tells us, *"By Him, all things were created."* Genesis, the book of beginnings, gives an accounting of what original creativity looked like. God created man in His image and inherent in that image is creativity. We are made in the image of a creator and within us is the both the desire and ability to create. Our creativity reflects the One in whose image

WHAT ARE YOU SENSING, SEEING, FEELING, OR HEARING FROM HIM?

_____

_____

_____

_____

_____

_____

_____

_____

_____

_____

_____

_____

_____

_____

_____

_____

we are made. When we create we are most like our Heavenly Father.

God is the Divine creator and His creativity built substance out of nothing. Out of His imagination and design He created a universe with its milky way, solar system, moons and planets, all centered around the sun and in perfect balance and purpose. Man has spent decades researching the universe God created, discovering its vast components. Man has learned about the speed of light or the sound barrier but he still hasn't found the sky's height or the ocean's depth.

Man's body uniquely created with uniform heart beats and breath, life and death, is also a center of discovery. People spend millions of dollars and man hours on development and scientific research to learn how to heal what God has created. Doctors call their profession "the practice of medicine."

God tells us in Proverbs 25:2, *"It is the Glory of God to conceal a matter; to search out a matter is the Glory of Kings."* Did you know that some of the most beautifully colored fish live in deepest parts of the ocean where there is no light? How about diamonds and gems or brilliant crystals formed inside the dark cavity of a mountainside? God hasn't hidden things *from* us; He has hidden them *for* us.

Some things appear to be similar in nature, yet God's designs are all one of a kind, individually and

WHAT ARE YOU SENSING, SEEING, FEELING, OR HEARING FROM HIM?

_____

_____

_____

_____

_____

_____

_____

_____

_____

_____

_____

_____

_____

_____

_____

_____

uniquely different. Each snowflake has a unique different shape and no two fingerprints are alike. If we put man's DNA into a computer, it produces an individual, unique sound; a song that is each our very own.

Creativity is more than an song, a picture, a dance, a word. Creativity demonstrates and replicates God's originality and creative power. Within our DNA, God placed the ability to create. When we tap into the treasures inside of us, our creativity merges with God's creativity. Paul called it "co-laboring" with Christ (2 Cor. 6:1), partnering in the work of Heaven. God's will co-laboring with man's will is seen in Genesis 2:19. God created the animals and then God gave Adam responsibility for naming them.

God didn't hang out and micro-manage Adam, give him hints or try to influence his decisions. God had full confidence in Adam's creative ability. Naming the animals was more significant than coming up with a word used to identify them. Naming the animals was assigning their character and nature. God created then Adam created. Together they displayed the model of co-laboring.

God created the original and we become imitators, illustrators of His nature, drawing attention to the true original. Man's creativity builds a bridge to reveal his creator, reflecting in whose image he is made.

WHAT ARE YOU SENSING, SEEING, FEELING, OR HEARING FROM HIM?

_____

_____

_____

_____

_____

_____

_____

_____

_____

_____

_____

_____

_____

_____

_____

_____

_____

The release of prophetic creativity is reflected in technology, politics, social reform, economics, engineering, science, medicine, government, architecture, math, exploration, psychiatry, pharmacy, botany, geology, science, as well as art, writing, dance, painting or drama.

Wisdom is the creative spirit of God. Read ahead what Proverbs says about wisdom. Note I have separated the sentences for easier reading.

"Counsel and sound judgment are mine; I have understanding and power."

"By me kings reign and rulers make laws that are just; by me princes govern, and all nobles who rule on earth. I love those who love me, and those who seek me find me."

"With me are riches and honor, enduring wealth and prosperity. My fruit is better than fine gold; what I yield surpasses choice silver. I walk in the way of righteousness, along the paths of justice, bestowing wealth on those who love me and making their treasuries full."

"The Lord brought me forth as the first of his works, before his deeds of old; I was appointed from eternity, from the beginning, before the world began. When there were no oceans, I was given birth, when there were no springs abounding with water; before the mountains were settled in place, before the hills, I was given birth, before he made the earth or its fields or any of the dust of the world."

"I was there when he set the heavens in place, when he marked out the horizon on the face of the deep, when he

WHAT ARE YOU SENSING, SEEING, FEELING, OR HEARING FROM HIM?

_____

_____

_____

_____

_____

_____

_____

_____

_____

_____

_____

_____

_____

_____

_____

_____

established the clouds above and fixed securely the fountains of the deep, when he gave the sea its boundary so the waters would not overstep his command, and when he marked out the foundations of the earth"

"Then I was the craftsman at his side. I was filled with delight day after day, rejoicing always in his presence, rejoicing in his whole world and delighting in mankind."

"Now then, my sons, listen to me; blessed are those who keep my ways. Listen to my instruction and be wise; do not ignore it. Blessed is the man who listens to me, watching daily at my doors, waiting at my doorway."

"For whoever finds me finds life and receives favor from the Lord. But whoever fails to find me harms himself; all who hate me love death." -Proverbs 8:14-36

Prophetic creativity is the partnership between creativity and wisdom as seen in the life of Solomon, who asked God for Wisdom according to 2Chron. 1:11. *"God said to Solomon, "Since this is your heart's desire and you have not asked for wealth, riches or honor, nor for the death of your enemies, and since you have not asked for a long life but for wisdom and knowledge to govern my people over whom I have made you king,"*

Note I separated the scriptural content into sentences for easier reading.

"God gave Solomon wisdom and very great insight, and a breadth of understanding as measureless as the sand on the seashore."

WHAT ARE YOU SENSING, SEEING, FEELING, OR HEARING FROM HIM?

_____

_____

_____

_____

_____

_____

_____

_____

_____

_____

_____

_____

_____

_____

_____

_____

"Solomon's wisdom was greater than the wisdom of all the men of the East, and greater than all the wisdom of Egypt. He was wiser than any other man, including Ethan the Ezrahite--wiser than Heman, Calcol and Darda, the sons of Mahol. And his fame spread to all the surrounding nations. He spoke three thousand proverbs and his songs numbered a thousand and five."

"He described plant life, from the cedar of Lebanon to the hyssop that grows out of walls. He also taught about animals and birds, reptiles and fish."

"Men of all nations came to listen to Solomon's wisdom, sent by all the kings of the world, who had heard of his wisdom." - 1Kings, 4:29-34

Pastor Bill Johnson says supernatural wisdom is both creative and prophetic. It can dismantle the obvious to see behind the scenes into the inner workings of a life, thought, concept, direction or design.

The religious spirit would like to silence every aspect of prophetic creativity in order to control. But God is calling His people to push out of the box of religious form and activity and begin to partner with the creative Spirit of Wisdom in order to demonstrate His raw power.

God placed within our design the ability to create. We contain creative DNA from our Heavenly Father. Jesus demonstrated this by using His spit (saliva) to heal someone!

WHAT ARE YOU SENSING, SEEING, FEELING, OR HEARING FROM HIM?

_____

_____

_____

_____

_____

_____

_____

_____

_____

_____

_____

_____

_____

_____

_____

_____

"After he took him aside, away from the crowd, Jesus put his fingers into the man's ears. Then he spit and touched the man's tongue. He looked up to heaven and with a deep sigh said to him, "Ephphatha!" (which means, "Be opened!"). At this, the man's ears were opened, his tongue was loosened and he began to speak plainly." (Mark 7:33-35)

Now I am not suggesting we begin a new type of anointing by the laying on of spit! However Jesus said all things were possible ... *"Jesus looked at them and said, "With man this is impossible, but with God all things are possible."* Matthew 19:26.

Inside each of us are treasures to be discovered. When we enter the gates of prophetic creativity, we access the hidden treasures and bring them into the light. When we co-labor with God we have access to His resources, strength and power. I like Hebrews 11:1 in the King James Version, *"Now faith is the substance of things hoped for, the evidence of things not seen."*

You enter the gates of prophetic creativity through faith. When we embrace prophetic creativity we set the atmosphere for creative miracles. That is, you call into existence that which was not previously seen. You reach into the Heavenly realm and you bring Heaven to earth...

WHAT ARE YOU SENSING, SEEING, FEELING, OR HEARING FROM HIM?

_____

_____

_____

_____

_____

_____

_____

_____

_____

_____

_____

_____

_____

_____

_____

_____

_____

Impartation for Prophetic Creativity

Put your hand on your chest and pray with me.

Papa, I ask you to forgive me for any way I hid, rejected or abandoned my talents and gifts. I break off every word ever spoken over me that would limit my creativity. I come out of agreement with a religious spirit that would not allow me freedom to express the gifts you have placed in me. Through Jesus Blood, I break the box of limitation.

You are calling me into my destiny and I receive your gift of creativity to be manifest in every aspect of my life. I ask for the Spirit of Wisdom to empower me and to empower creativity in it's fullest. I release a greater awareness and revelation of your Presence living in me.

I dedicate my gifts and abilities back to you. I ask you to revive the ideas and dreams that were deposited. I ask you to give me new dreams and visions...

Continue with your own prayer.....

_____
_____
_____
_____
_____
_____

WHAT ARE YOU SENSING, SEEING, FEELING, OR HEARING FROM HIM?

_____

_____

_____

_____

_____

_____

_____

_____

_____

_____

_____

_____

_____

_____

_____

CHAPTER 3

GATES OF
PROPHETIC DECLARATION

Nothing happens in the Kingdom without first a declaration is made. In Genesis God declared and existence, as we know it, began. God formed our world with His words. When God spoke He demonstrated the power of prophetic declaration. Prophetic declaration was God's first creative act!

The power of declaration is seen when Jesus spoke *"and rebuked the winds and the waves and it was completely calm"* (Matthew 8:26).

WHAT ARE YOU SENSING, SEEING, FEELING, OR HEARING FROM HIM?

_____

_____

_____

_____

_____

_____

_____

_____

_____

_____

_____

_____

_____

_____

_____

_____

_____

Jesus also spoke *"in a loud voice, Lazarus, come out,"* calling Lazarus back to life from the grave (John 11:43)   and on another occasion Jesus spoke to a young man who had died, telling him to "get up" and *"the dead man sat up and began to talk"* (Luke 7:15). Jesus modeled prophetic declaration so we would have first hand revelation of the creative power of words.

We were foster parents to our youngest child who was ten days old when she came to live with us and from the moment we saw her we wanted to adopt her. She was not in good health and for two years we loved and took care of her. There were lots of factors the courts were considering with regard to her future. For each court hearing, I had to be prepared to release her if the judge ordered her to return to biological family members petitioning the court for custody. Four times in a row, the hearing was either postponed or changed for some reason. It felt like an emotional roller coaster. However, the judge made it clear that at the next hearing he would be making a final determination.

I shared my anxiousness and uncertainty with a friend who prayed for me and then looked directly into my eyes and made a bold declaration. She said firmly, *"this child is yours."* This was 1987 and at the time I didn't understand prophetic declaration, but when she looked at me and spoke, something in her voice filled my spirit and boosted my faith. I began to come into agreement with my friend's faith

WHAT ARE YOU SENSING, SEEING, FEELING, OR HEARING FROM HIM?

_____

_____

_____

_____

_____

_____

_____

_____

_____

_____

_____

_____

_____

_____

_____

_____

and rather than beg God to allow us to adopt her, we spoke over her and out loud *"this child is ours!"*

A few months later we received notice of the new court date. One week before the hearing, we also received a phone call from the family members who was opposing our adoption asking for a private meeting without the attorneys. At the meeting they said they were Christians and that the Lord had told them not to fight our adoption. They said these exact words, "The Lord told us *this child is yours*." Then went on to tell us they were withdrawing their petition for custody.

When the adoption was final the judge made a declaration as well. He declared that she would receive our name and have all the rights and privilege of a natural child with full benefits of inheritance!

I believed my friend had a real connection with God. He answered her prayer and my respect for her was upgraded and I yearned to have that kind of faith. Now I realize her faith was connected to her authority in Him. She spoke a word of knowledge through a prophetic declaration. Her authority in the Kingdom partnered with obedience to God's word of knowledge to her. Together, the words created what was not yet in existence.

Before I understood the power of declaration my prayers consisted of asking God to come and do what Jesus already gave me authority to do.

WHAT ARE YOU SENSING, SEEING, FEELING, OR HEARING FROM HIM?

_____

_____

_____

_____

_____

_____

_____

_____

_____

_____

_____

_____

_____

_____

_____

_____

I needed just to agree and partner with God's word in the Bible, and His word to me personally. For example, when someone in my family was sick, I would intercede and ask God to come and heal them. Over the years, I saw so very few people healed I almost stopped praying for healing believing the greater miracle would be God answering my prayer! I attributed the lack of victory to my lack of faith or some unknown area of sin that needed to be dealt with before God would answer my prayers. Consequently, most of my prayer time turned inward, focusing on my unbelief and asking God to show me where I had failed Him. Worse yet, I began to believe that maybe it wasn't God's will for people to be healed.

Thank you to people like Germaine Copeland (Prayers That Avail Much) and Beth Moore (Praying God's Word) and others who helped us to learn how to effectively pray the word of God. Praying the Lords prayer (Matthew 6:9-13) was one of the pivotal turning points in my faith. These forerunners brought to our attention Hebrews 4:12 *"God's word is alive and powerful, sharper than a two-edged sword."*

From the place of rest and faith in the accomplished work of Jesus' death, blood and resurrection, prophetic declaration is partnering with God's word. Jesus commissioned His followers (this includes you and me) to *"Heal the sick, raise the dead, cleanse those who have leprosy, drive out demons. Freely you have received, freely give"* (Matthew 10:8).

WHAT ARE YOU SENSING, SEEING, FEELING, OR HEARING FROM HIM?

_____

_____

_____

_____

_____

_____

_____

_____

_____

_____

_____

_____

_____

_____

_____

_____

In Luke 9:2 Jesus *"sent them out to preach the kingdom of God and to heal the sick."* And in Luke 10:9, *"Heal the sick who are there and tell them, the kingdom of God is near you."*

We pray with declaration to exercise our authority as Jesus commissioned. Our declarations unlock Heaven and Heaven's power is released.

In a recent meeting there were several words of knowledge about back's being healed. When the invitation was given for people to come up who had back problems, our team partnered with God's word and released healing power. Almost everyone who received prayer was healed. One man who had a crushed foot came forward and after healing prayer all the pain was gone and he could walk with full weight on the healed foot. A lady with crutches was fully able to walk without them and without pain.

Watching God work through healing prayer was my introduction to prophetic declaration. I still don't see 100% of those I pray for be healed but the more I press in to declare healing the more I see results.

Healing prayer is just one aspect of declaration. There were a group of us who had gathered together for a 24-hour HOP (House of Prayer.)

During that meeting we began to call out loud the names of those in our family we had concern for. We turned to face the north, south, east, and west and

WHAT ARE YOU SENSING, SEEING, FEELING, OR HEARING FROM HIM?

_____

_____

_____

_____

_____

_____

_____

_____

_____

_____

_____

_____

_____

_____

_____

_____

_____

with each turn, we made our declarations, speaking the names and calling them "home." I joined with the group, calling out my brother's name. The history was my brother had not been in contact with anyone in our family for almost 10 years. We actually had no idea where he was or if he was still alive. Two days after the 24-hour HOP my brother contacted me.

Another personal breakthrough happened while I was in my first year at Bethel School of Supernatural Ministry. We had a property for sale and the escrow cancelled due to an error in the issuance of a county permit. In the meantime we didn't want to lose the house we were purchasing so we went ahead and closed our new escrow believing the property permit problem would be easy to resolve. Well, you can guess what happened! It wasn't a simple problem to resolve and the property needed to be taken off the market during the process.

We made double house payments until we exhausted our savings account. I was pretty embarrassed attending a supernatural school of ministry and drowning in a financial ocean. I was almost ready to leave school and go back to work full time when Pastor Bill Johnson (Bethel Church) spoke on prophetic declaration. The challenge was before me. I could shrink back to mediocrity or I could press in and just try it.

Not sure what my declaration was supposed to look like, this is what I wrote.

WHAT ARE YOU SENSING, SEEING, FEELING, OR HEARING FROM HIM?

_____

_____

_____

_____

_____

_____

_____

_____

_____

_____

_____

_____

_____

_____

_____

_____

My Decree

I will not look at circumstances.
I will stay focused on God.
Send the resources of Heaven –
release the Blessing on my finances.
I bind the enemy of despair, depression,
desperation, d-day, all the d's are DEFEATED.

Discouragement, disillusionment, decrease, doom,
death, d-days … be gone – gone – gone –
you're bound – you're sent off.
I drink from the well of life,
there is no turning back.

I DECLARE provision and resources,
fruit of Heaven come down, supplies increase.
Break through – break through – break through
break through – break through!

I align myself with Heaven.
Health is mine – prosperity is mine.
I am an over-comer, a princess, an heir and
co-heir with Christ.
I am a victor – complete in Him, lacking nothing.

NO Good THING will be withheld from me.
I sit in Heavenly Places with Christ and He has given
me all authority.
I have favor — the favor of God.

WHAT ARE YOU SENSING, SEEING, FEELING, OR HEARING FROM HIM?

_____

_____

_____

_____

_____

_____

_____

_____

_____

_____

_____

_____

_____

_____

_____

Favor is continually extended toward me.
The face of God is turned toward me.
I am precious, the apple of His eye.
I am loved beyond measure.
Mercy is my pillow at night and
love is my blanket.
Grace is my bed to rest upon.
The window of Heaven is opened in my direction.

The blood was shed. The war is won,
I have the Victory. It is mine. I take it. I own it.

I posted copies of My Decree where I'd be reminded to read it out loud. While nothing happened right away with regard to our finances, I felt l was being pro-active. Two weeks later I left for a mission trip to Mexico. The day before I was to return home, I called my husband and he exclaimed "I have good news, the property sold with a 30 day escrow."

Prophetic declarations are powerful and set a course in motion. The positive side is our words have the power to call out the treasure in someone, the power to heal, even the power to shift the atmosphere and bring in the light of Heaven. The down side is when prophetic declaration is used to control or bully or to puff up the one with the microphone, it can set fear into motion. James tells us the tongue is a small part of the body, but compares it with a small spark that can cause a great forest fire (James 3:5.) We have

WHAT ARE YOU SENSING, SEEING, FEELING, OR HEARING FROM HIM?

_____

_____

_____

_____

_____

_____

_____

_____

_____

_____

_____

_____

_____

_____

_____

_____

_____

all heard a fire alarm and had to discern if there really was a fire, or just an alarm going off!

Proverbs 18:21 says "The tongue has the power of life and death..." Let's commit to strengthen, encourage and comfort and thereby, partner with the power that brings life.

Do you have an area that needs God's help and intervention? Your greatest obstacle mirrors your highest call so go ahead and take action. If you need some "power points," here is a list of scriptures reflecting YOUR inheritance!!

- I am complete in Him who is the Head of all principality and power (Colossians 2:10).

- I am alive with Christ (Ephesians 2:5).

- I am free from the law of sin and death (Romans 8:2).

- I am far from oppression, and fear does not come near me (Isaiah 54:14).

- I am born of God, and the evil one does not touch me (I John 5:18).

- I am holy and without blame before Him in love (I Peter 1:16; Ephesians 1:4).

- I have the peace of God that passes all understanding (Philippians 4:7).

WHAT ARE YOU SENSING, SEEING, FEELING, OR HEARING FROM HIM?

_____

_____

_____

_____

_____

_____

_____

_____

_____

_____

_____

_____

_____

_____

_____

_____

- I have the Greater One living in me; greater is He Who is in me than he who is in the world (I John 4:4).

- I have the mind of Christ (Philippians 2:5; I Corinthians 2:16).

- I have received the gift of righteousness and reign as a king in life by Jesus Christ (Romans 5:17).

- I have no lack for my God supplies all of my need according to His riches in glory by Christ Jesus (Philippians 4:19).

- I have received the spirit of wisdom and revelation in the knowledge of Jesus, the eyes of my understanding being enlightened (Ephesians 1:17,18).

- I have received the power of the Holy Spirit to lay hands on the sick and see them recover, to cast out demons, to speak with new tongues. I have power over all the power of the enemy, and nothing shall by any means harm me (Mark 16:17,18; Luke 10:17,19).

- I have put off the old man and have put on the new man, which is renewed in the knowledge after the image of Him Who created me (Colossians 3:9,10).

WHAT ARE YOU SENSING, SEEING, FEELING, OR HEARING FROM HIM?

_____

_____

_____

_____

_____

_____

_____

_____

_____

_____

_____

_____

_____

_____

_____

_____

- I have given, and it is given to me; good measure, pressed down, shaken together, and running over, men give into my bosom (Luke 6:38).

- I can quench all the fiery darts of the wicked one with my shield of faith (Ephesians 6:16).

- I can do all things through Christ Jesus (Philippians 4:13).

- I shall do even greater works than Christ Jesus (John 14:12).

- I show forth the praises of God Who has called me out of darkness into His marvelous light (I Peter 2:9).

- I am God's child for I am born again of the incorruptible seed of the Word of God, which lives and abides forever (I Peter 1:23).

- I am God's workmanship, created in Christ unto good works (Ephesians 2:10).

- I am a new creature in Christ (II Corinthians 5:17).

- I am a spirit being alive to God (I Thessalonians 5:23; Romans 6:11).

WHAT ARE YOU SENSING, SEEING, FEELING, OR HEARING FROM HIM?

_____

_____

_____

_____

_____

_____

_____

_____

_____

_____

_____

_____

_____

_____

_____

- I am a believer, and the light of the Gospel shines in my mind (II Corinthians 4:4).

- I am a doer of the Word and blessed in my actions (James 1:22,25).

- I am the light of the world (Matthew 5:14).

- I am a joint-heir with Christ (Romans 8:17).

- I am more than a conqueror through Him Who loves me (Romans 8:37).

- I am an overcomer by the blood of the Lamb and the word of my testimony (Revelation 12:11).

- I am a partaker of His divine nature (II Peter 1:3,4).

- I am an ambassador for Christ (II Corinthians 5:20).

- I am part of a chosen generation, a royal priesthood, a holy nation, a purchased people (I Peter 2:9).

- I am the righteousness of God in Jesus Christ (II Corinthians 5:21).

- I am the temple of the Holy Spirit; I am not my own (I Corinthians 6:19).

WHAT ARE YOU SENSING, SEEING, FEELING, OR HEARING FROM HIM?

_____

_____

_____

_____

_____

_____

_____

_____

_____

_____

_____

_____

_____

_____

_____

_____

_____

- I am the head and not the tail; I am above only and not beneath (Deuteronomy 28:13).

- I am His elect, full of mercy, kindness, humility, and longsuffering (Romans 8:33; Colossians 3:12).

- I am forgiven of all my sins and washed in the Blood (Ephesians 1:7).

- I am delivered from the power of darkness and translated into God's kingdom (Colossians 1:13).

- I am redeemed from the curse of sin, sickness, and poverty (Galatians 3:13; Deuteronomy 28:15-68).

- I am firmly rooted, built up, established in my faith and overflowing with gratitude (Colossians 2:7).

- I am called of God to be the voice of His praise (II Timothy 1:9; Psalm 66:8).

- I am healed by the stripes of Jesus (I Peter 2:24; Isaiah 53:5).

- I am raised up with Christ and seated in heavenly places (Colossians 2:12; Ephesians 2:6).

WHAT ARE YOU SENSING, SEEING, FEELING, OR HEARING FROM HIM?

_____

_____

_____

_____

_____

_____

_____

_____

_____

_____

_____

_____

_____

_____

_____

_____

- I am greatly loved by God (Colossians 3:12; Romans 1:7; I Thessalonians 1:4; Ephesians 2:4).

- I am strengthened with all might according to His glorious power (Colossians 1:11).

- I am submitted to God, and the devil flees from me because I resist him in the Name of Jesus (James 4:7).

- It is not I who live, but Christ lives in me (Galatians 2:20).

- I press on toward the goal to win the prize to which God in Christ Jesus is calling us upward (Philippians 3:14).

- For God has not given us a spirit of fear; but of power, love, and a sound mind (II Timothy 1:7).

- It is for freedom He has set me free (Galatians5:1).

If needed, ask God to forgive you for any mistakes or sin and accept His forgiveness. Then in confidence and faith make your prophetic declaration now…

WHAT ARE YOU SENSING, SEEING, FEELING, OR HEARING FROM HIM?

_____

_____

_____

_____

_____

_____

_____

_____

_____

_____

_____

_____

_____

_____

_____

_____

_____

_____

My Decree

_____

_____

_____

_____

_____

_____

_____

_____

_____

_____

_____

_____

_____

_____

_____

_____

_____

_____

_____

_____

_____

WHAT ARE YOU SENSING, SEEING, FEELING, OR HEARING FROM HIM?

_____

_____

_____

_____

_____

_____

_____

_____

_____

_____

_____

_____

_____

_____

_____

_____

_____

CHAPTER 4

GATES OF
PROPHETIC ACTS

Prophetic acts are faith in physical motion. Christian practices of taking communion, water baptism, laying on of hands for healing, anointing with oil, raising our arms during worship and even kneeling in prayer are all prophetic acts. Prophetic acts are extensions of our faith physically positioning us in partnership with God.

WHAT ARE YOU SENSING, SEEING, FEELING, OR HEARING FROM HIM?

_____

_____

_____

_____

_____

_____

_____

_____

_____

_____

_____

_____

_____

_____

_____

Moses faith to physically partner with the supernatural power of God is recorded in Exodus. Moses "*stretched out his hand over the sea and all that night the Lord drove the sea back with a strong east wind and turned it into dry land. The waters were divided and the Israelites went through the sea on dry ground, with a wall of water on their right and on their left*" (Exodus 14:21,22).

Then it happened again in Exodus 14:26,27 when the Lord said to Moses "*Stretch out your hand over the sea so that the waters may flow back over the Egyptians and their chariots and horsemen. Moses stretched out his hand over the sea, and at daybreak the sea went back to its place.*" Moses partnered through obedience with God's word and participated in one of the most astonishing miracles recorded in scripture.

The fall of the walls of Jericho in Joshua 6:20 is another miracle resulting from an obedient action in partnership with God's word. "*When the trumpets sounded, the people shouted, and at the sound of the trumpet, when the people gave a loud shout, the wall collapsed; so every man charged straight in, and they took the city.*"

Jesus often touched those He healed or ask them to activate their healing by physically doing something that partnered with Jesus words of healing.

- Jesus heals Peter's mother in law who had a high fever when <u>he took her by the hand and helped her to sit up</u> (Matthew 8:15).

WHAT ARE YOU SENSING, SEEING, FEELING, OR HEARING FROM HIM?

_____

_____

_____

_____

_____

_____

_____

_____

_____

_____

_____

_____

_____

_____

_____

_____

- A paralyzed man is healed when he obeys Jesus by <u>picking up his mat</u> and going home" (Matthew 9:6,7).

- Jesus <u>makes a mud pie with his spit</u> (here is the spit again!) and <u>placed it on the man's eyes</u> and then tells the blind man to go wash in a pool of water. *"So the man <u>went and washed</u>, and came home seeing"* (John 9:7).

I have learned value of asking the Lord what He wants to show me about the person seeking healing *before* beginning to pray for them. The Lord may reveal the root of the injury or if there is emotional or body trauma. It is usually during the time I am waiting for Him to show me how to pray when I would receive the impression to do a prophetic act. This information would change the way I might pray.

In addition, the Lord might confirm through an impression to lay hands on the injured area or maybe the heart area for emotional trauma. I might speak to their body, their heart, their mind, to a spiritual influence or ask them about forgiveness. Remember the importance of always asking permission before touching someone and use appropriate boundaries to honor the person seeking prayer.

After praying, ask the person to activate their healing by doing something they couldn't do before. After praying for the person with a crushed foot, we

WHAT ARE YOU SENSING, SEEING, FEELING, OR HEARING FROM HIM?

_____

_____

_____

_____

_____

_____

_____

_____

_____

_____

_____

_____

_____

_____

_____

_____

ask him to try to rotate the foot or point his toes. The physical action put his faith in motion.

A lady came forward for prayer and while she was talking about her chronic back pain the Lord showed me a spirit wrapped around her spine. He showed me she was a missionary in a foreign land and had encountered witchcraft. Without saying anything to her I reached behind her while I was praying for her back to be healed. I moved my hand symbolically unwrapping the binding from her spine and discarding the binding. I also asked her to pray to forgive and break any spiritual ties with the people of that land. I didn't need to tell her what I *saw in the spirit*, rather just asked if she had been a missionary in a particular land. When she said "yes" that was my cue to move forward with the word the Lord gave me and pray for her back to be healed at the same time doing the prophetic act. Her back was healed and she felt "released" and said she felt like "something left her." It did!

Someone with a stiff neck came up for prayer and the Lord revealed to us there were burdens he was carrying that weren't his. Before praying for healing, I invited him to ask God to forgive him for taking on responsibilities that weren't his and he complied. During prayer for healing I physically brushed off his upper back with my hands to remove the heavy burdens and commanded his neck be healed. He gained full movement in his neck and felt "lighter."

WHAT ARE YOU SENSING, SEEING, FEELING, OR HEARING FROM HIM?

_____

_____

_____

_____

_____

_____

_____

_____

_____

_____

_____

_____

_____

_____

_____

_____

_____

Our prayers for healing always conclude with asking the person to do a prophetic act by trying something they couldn't do before they were prayed for. If they have feel improvement we press in again for complete healing. Each time we will ask them to try something they couldn't do before. With any improvement, we thank God and press in for 100% healing by praying again.

Other types of prophetic acts I have either seen or participated with are:

- Repent over the sins of a land and place a stake in the ground with scriptures of blessing.

- Anoint a prayer cloth and give it to someone who is sick to keep in their shoe or place under their pillow.

- Write scripture on the framework of a building before completing construction.

- Use banners, flags, and worship arts to proclaim God's reign.

- Paint during worship as a form of worship.

- Apply anointing oil to door knobs, door frames and windows.

- Prayer walk through a neighborhood and proclaim the goodness of God; bless the people and call them home to His heart.

WHAT ARE YOU SENSING, SEEING, FEELING, OR HEARING FROM HIM?

_____

_____

_____

_____

_____

_____

_____

_____

_____

_____

_____

_____

_____

_____

_____

_____

- Memorialize a place of victory.

- Visit a mountain top and worship over a community.

- Ask forgiveness and burn an occult related object .

- Wash someone's feet to remove the "dust" they carry from places that rejected them.

- Blow the shofar.

- Clap my hands loudly to shift the atmosphere.

- Place a crown, shield, veil, ring, robe, shoes or sword

A child died due to the skull never completely closing, leaving a very large soft spot gap under the scalp. When a second baby was born with the same issue and without money for doctors her family gave up hope and didn't name her. Mom and dad brought the baby for prayer. My friend, Erica began to pray for the child and with a prophetic act she motioned as if to close up the gap. They declared healing while simultaneously prophetically closing the gap. The parents and team broke out in dancing and laughter as they watched the skull underneath the scalp almost completely close. The parents named the baby after the girl who prayed for her.

WHAT ARE YOU SENSING, SEEING, FEELING, OR HEARING FROM HIM?

_____

_____

_____

_____

_____

_____

_____

_____

_____

_____

_____

_____

_____

_____

_____

_____

Word spread around this small community and other mothers brought sick babies. The team placed the hand of the healed baby on the sick babies and several other babies were healed.

Creativity partnered with prophetic declaration and prophetic acts and the results were several miracles of healing and a whole bunch of happy parents!

After praying about 10 minutes for Norma, who had significant hearing loss, one team member prayed and snapped their fingers near her ear as a prophetic act. Norma jolted. We apologized not meaning to startle her. She laughed and said "I couldn't hear anything out of that ear and I *heard* the snap!" Her hearing was restored.

Heidi Baker (Iris Ministries) shared a testimony of a man who didn't have a knee cap. As Heidi prayed, the Lord gave her a picture of His spare body parts in Heaven! She felt He was giving her access to what she needed. While praying, Heidi she lifted her hand toward heaven and prophetically took a knee cap and placed it on the man's defective knee. Suddenly he had a knee cap and full mobility of his knee! These are the kind of testimonies that keep us pressing in for more.

During a counseling session, one of my clients talked about being verbally assaulted. In the spirit, I saw several daggers still lodged in her back just about the time she said, "I feel they stabbed me in the back."

WHAT ARE YOU SENSING, SEEING, FEELING, OR HEARING FROM HIM?

_____

_____

_____

_____

_____

_____

_____

_____

_____

_____

_____

_____

_____

_____

_____

_____

_____

_____

I led her through prayers of forgiveness and she broke soul ties and word curses. Then I began to prophetically dislodge and remove the daggers and gently rub those spots asking the Lord to send His healing oil to sooth and comfort. She felt the dysfunctional connection with her family dissolve and felt His peace.

In a healing meeting the Lord highlighted a man and I had a prophetic word for him about his joy being restored and I saw him jogging. I walked over to him and immediately the Holy Spirit visited and both of us began to laugh. Well, it was one of those Holy Spirit laughter times and several people around us began to laugh, too. He was doubled over laughing and tears were rolling down his cheeks! The next day his wife told me he had Parkinson's and hadn't been able to sleep through the night in months. She said after the meeting he slept all through the night and in the morning had no pain or tremors in his legs. The presence of the Lord shifted the atmosphere and was a catalyst for healing.

Jesus stilled the waves and wind through declaration which resulted in a shifting of the physical atmospheric condition. The illustration has a spiritual application as well. Jesus presence shifts spiritual atmospheres from darkness to light; from chaos to calm.

Music and movies present powerful atmospheres. Those atmospheres can cause you to laugh or cry; to feel peace or feel fear. Spiritual atmospheres

WHAT ARE YOU SENSING, SEEING, FEELING, OR HEARING FROM HIM?

_____

_____

_____

_____

_____

_____

_____

_____

_____

_____

_____

_____

_____

_____

_____

_____

_____

are discernable and can be shifted by changing the channel and bringing in God's presence. One simple example is when we feel sad or lonely and put on praise or worship music to lift our spirit. Praise shifts the atmosphere because He inhabits the praises of His people.

His presence shifts the atmosphere and we carry His presence! We can shift the atmosphere when we bring His presence into a situation. During a recent support group we were talking about some of the tragic circumstances the ladies had experienced. There was a heaviness that fell in the room and I felt it, too. Discerning it was a spirit of fear, I asked the ladies to stand and put their hand on their chest and verbally partner with the Lord's peace that passes understanding. We thanked the Lord that He had brought us healing and we declared His goodness. Within a few minutes we could feel the heaviness leave and the ladies faces were brighter.

What we focus on we empower. Through a prophetic act we turned our focus and partnered with God and He met us in that place.

Make a list of prophetic acts you have done.

_____

_____

_____

_____

_____

WHAT ARE YOU SENSING, SEEING, FEELING, OR HEARING FROM HIM?

_____

_____

_____

_____

_____

_____

_____

_____

_____

_____

_____

_____

_____

_____

_____

_____

_____

_____

_____

_____

_____

_____

Make a list of some of the prophetic acts the Lord is showing you to try.

_____

_____

_____

_____

_____

_____

_____

_____

_____

_____

_____

_____

_____

_____

_____

_____

_____

WHAT ARE YOU SENSING, SEEING, FEELING, OR HEARING FROM HIM?

_____

_____

_____

_____

_____

_____

_____

_____

_____

_____

_____

_____

_____

_____

_____

_____

_____

CHAPTER 5

GATES OF
PROPHETIC INTERCESSION

Intercessors were often a misunderstood peculiar people who felt, sensed, heard, or saw the things of God yet were not always able to be part of an apostolic or prophetic covering blessing and encouraging them. Laboring in prayer, intercessors identified with roles of priests, praying on behalf of the people to

WHAT ARE YOU SENSING, SEEING, FEELING, OR HEARING FROM HIM?

_____

_____

_____

_____

_____

_____

_____

_____

_____

_____

_____

_____

_____

_____

_____

_____

_____

_____

God, and prophets, praying on behalf of God to the people. Focusing on spiritual warfare and problem solving, they were heavy burdened and tired, seeing little fruit from their long hours before the Lord. Rather than seeking God in how to pray more effectively, prayer was focused from a defensive position of fear and striving seeking to divert what the devil was doing.

Intercession becomes easy and effective when we enter into relationship and intimacy with Papa God. This Psalm reflects our heart's cry. *"Whom have I in heaven but you? And earth has nothing I desire besides you. My flesh and my heart may fail, but God is the strength of my heart and my portion forever"* (Psalm 73:25,26).

Once we enter the depth of His love and presence, He shows us His desires. From extreme intense love for the Father and His children, we capture Heaven's heartbeat.

I like to call intercession "receiving blue prints from Heaven!" That is, receiving His plans for nations, regions, business, or peoples lives. Partnering in agreement with what He shows us, we declare or pray it into our world. In this way we pray from His heart and call into existence the desires that are already in the heart of God, Being sensitive to the Holy Spirit, we lay down our and agendas and striving. The only way we can do this is to understand the Heavenly

WHAT ARE YOU SENSING, SEEING, FEELING, OR HEARING FROM HIM?

_____

_____

_____

_____

_____

_____

_____

_____

_____

_____

_____

_____

_____

_____

_____

_____

_____

realms and their influence on our prophetic gifting. In Genesis there are at least three references to the plural "Heavens."

Gen. 1:1, *"In the beginning God created the heavens and the earth."*

Gen 2:1, *"Thus the heavens and the earth were completed in all their vast array."*

Gen 2:4, *"This is the account of the heavens and the earth when they were created. When the Lord God made the earth and the heavens."*

And in Deuteronomy 14:14, *"To the Lord your God belong the heavens, even the highest heavens, the earth and everything in it."*

And in 1Kings 8:27, "But will God really dwell on earth? The heavens, even the highest heaven, cannot contain you. How much less this temple I have built!"

These verses as well as 2 Chronicles 6:18, Nehimiah 9:6, and Psalm 115:16 all refer to the plural *"heavens."*

Three Heavenly realms are shown us in scripture. The term "realm" according to Encarta Dictionary of North America, is defined as "an area or domain." Realms can be regions, spheres or areas of dominion.

The first heaven is identified in Revelation 21:1, *"Then I saw a new heaven and a new earth, for the*

WHAT ARE YOU SENSING, SEEING, FEELING, OR HEARING FROM HIM?

_____

_____

_____

_____

_____

_____

_____

_____

_____

_____

_____

_____

_____

_____

first heaven and the first earth had passed away, and there was no longer any sea." This is the earthly realm that encompasses our cities, buildings, and bodies and the physical realm in which we breathe, walk, and work.

The second heaven is identified in Revelation 14:6, *"And I saw another angel flying in midheaven, having an eternal gospel to preach to those who live on the earth and to every nation and tribe and tongue and people"* (NASB). Daniel (Daniel 10:13) spoke of this realm through a vision of demonic and angelic war.

The third heaven is described by Paul in 2 Corinthians 12:2-4, *"I know a man in Christ who fourteen years ago was caught up to the third heaven. Whether it was in the body or out of the body I do not know. God knows. And I know that this man-whether in the body or apart from the body I do not know, but God knows, was caught up to paradise. He heard inexpressible things, things that man is not permitted to tell."*

Paul correlates his third heaven experience with paradise (vs. 4) and describes this realm where he heard *"inexpressible things, things that man is not permitted to tell."* Paul experienced himself *"caught up"* in a place with God similar to what we see in Ephesians 2:6,7 being *"raised us up with Christ and seated us with him in the heavenly realms in Christ Jesus, in order that in the coming ages he might show the incomparable riches of his grace, expressed in his kindness to us in Christ Jesus."*

WHAT ARE YOU SENSING, SEEING, FEELING, OR HEARING FROM HIM?

_____

_____

_____

_____

_____

_____

_____

_____

_____

_____

_____

_____

_____

_____

_____

_____

_____

Prophetic people can discern activity from all three Heavenly realms but discernment alone shouldn't be the criteria for prayerful intercession.

Jesus is our example and He prayed from the third Heaven realm. He told us in John 5:19, *"Jesus gave them this answer: "I tell you the truth, the Son can do nothing by himself; he can do only what he sees his Father doing, because whatever the Father does the Son also does."*

Our prophetic antennae will access the supernatural through the Holy Spirit to help us determine the direction for prayer. If we are premature in our efforts, we can miss the heart of Papa God.

Discernment and prayer focus:

1. First Heaven– Discern personalities, body language, lifestyles, logic and reason.

    • Prayer is from a human perspective.

2. Second Heaven – Discern demonic spiritual activity, oppression, depression, fear and doom and darkness.

    • Prayer is to find the devil and stop him.

3. Third Heaven – Discern angelic activity, God's love and joy, access heartbeat of Papa God.

    • Prayer is to implement the blue prints of Heaven.

WHAT ARE YOU SENSING, SEEING, FEELING, OR HEARING FROM HIM?

_____

_____

_____

_____

_____

_____

_____

_____

_____

_____

_____

_____

_____

_____

_____

_____

Let's take a multiple choice quiz. Which of the above Heavenly realms do you think would be the most effective partnership in prayer? _____

I picked #3 and I am sure you did, too!

David's Psalm27 gives us a glimpse into what third Heaven prayer looks like.

"The Lord is my light and my salvation-- whom shall I fear? The Lord is the stronghold of my life-- of whom shall I be afraid?

When evil men advance against me to devour my flesh, when my enemies and my foes attack me, they will stumble and fall.

Though an army besiege me, my heart will not fear; though war break out against me, even then will I be confident.

One thing I ask of the Lord, this is what I seek: that I may dwell in the house of the Lord all the days of my life, to gaze upon the beauty of the Lord and to seek him in his temple.

For in the day of trouble he will keep me safe in his dwelling; he will hide me in the shelter of his tabernacle and set me high upon a rock.

Then my head will be exalted above the enemies who surround me; at his tabernacle will I sacrifice with shouts of joy; I will sing and make music to the Lord.

WHAT ARE YOU SENSING, SEEING, FEELING, OR HEARING FROM HIM?

_____

_____

_____

_____

_____

_____

_____

_____

_____

_____

_____

_____

_____

_____

_____

_____

Hear my voice when I call, O Lord; be merciful to me and answer me.

My heart says of you, "Seek his face!" Your face, Lord, I will seek."

David, who lived before Christ and His Cross, knew how, in the day of trouble, to access the Kingdom of God, dwell in His house, gaze upon His beauty, and seek Him in His temple and enter the shelter of His tabernacle and be set high upon a rock AND with shouts of joy, sing to the Lord!

How much more should we, who have received our full inheritance of the Kingdom through Jesus be able to dwell in AND pray from a place of strength in the finished work of the Cross! *"For through him we both have access to the Father by one Spirit. Consequently, you are no longer foreigners and aliens, but fellow citizens with God's people and members of God's household, built on the foundation of the apostles and prophets, with Christ Jesus himself as the chief cornerstone"* (Ephesians 2:18-20).

Intercessors press in to God and release prophetic creativity, prophetic declaration, and prophetic acts. Intercessors appeared weird before being weird was popular! Thank goodness, someone broke out of the prayer closet and started dancing!

WHAT ARE YOU SENSING, SEEING, FEELING, OR HEARING FROM HIM?

_____

_____

_____

_____

_____

_____

_____

_____

_____

_____

_____

_____

_____

_____

_____

_____

Prophetic Intercession Exercise

Think of a difficult situation you or someone you know is facing.

With that situation in mind, what are you discerning from the three Heavenly realms?

1. First Heaven: The problem

_____
_____
_____
_____
_____
_____
_____
_____
_____
_____
_____
_____

2. Second Heaven: The obstacle

_____
_____
_____
_____
_____

WHAT ARE YOU SENSING, SEEING, FEELING, OR HEARING FROM HIM?

_____

_____

_____

_____

_____

_____

_____

_____

_____

_____

_____

_____

_____

_____

_____

_____

_____

_____

_____

_____

_____

_____

_____

3. Third Heaven: The solution

Before you assume you know, or access your personal agenda, seek the Lord by entering into His presence and wait for Him to show you what He would want for the situation. For example: *"Papa God, what is your heart for this situation? What is the destiny you have for those involved (could be nations, cities, or individuals)?"*

_____

_____

_____

_____

_____

_____

_____

_____

_____

_____

WHAT ARE YOU SENSING, SEEING, FEELING, OR HEARING FROM HIM?

_____

_____

_____

_____

_____

_____

_____

_____

_____

_____

_____

_____

_____

_____

_____

_____

_____

_____

_____

_____

_____

_____

After you have a sense of what Papa God is telling or showing you, go ahead and write your prayer partnering with Heaven.

_____

_____

_____

_____

_____

_____

_____

_____

_____

_____

_____

_____

_____

_____

_____

WHAT ARE YOU SENSING, SEEING, FEELING, OR HEARING FROM HIM?

_____

_____

_____

_____

_____

_____

_____

_____

_____

_____

_____

_____

_____

_____

_____

_____

_____

_____

CHAPTER 6

GATES OF
PROPHETIC EVANGELISM

When people met Jesus they were saved, healed and delivered through an experiential encounter. Today's evangelistic outreaches look much different from former days of door knocking, handing out tracts and street preaching.

Supernatural evangelism is centered in prophecy that strengthens, encourages, and comforts speaks

WHAT ARE YOU SENSING, SEEING, FEELING, OR HEARING FROM HIM?

_____

_____

_____

_____

_____

_____

_____

_____

_____

_____

_____

_____

_____

truth. Words of wisdom and knowledge reveal physical, emotional, and spiritual conflicts and give us access to deeper issues of the heart. The demonstration of Jesus' power reveals His Glory according to John 2:11 and when His Glory is revealed He draws people to Himself.

Everyone is a candidate for God's love. Supernatural evangelism reveals the extravagant heart of God. There is an old saying that people don't care how much you know until they know how much you care. Prophetic evangelism's personal touch centers in relationship rather than religious form.

We set up a table in the park with a sign that said, *Encouraging Words!* As people approached, we'd ask God to reveal something about them that would open the door for ministry. Often we would be shown a physical problem and press in for healing. "How did you know that," they'd ask. What a great introduction to the One who knows them best and loves them the most!

Tony, my husband, has relationship with musicians. The venue has a small café and we go early to have dinner or coffee. We purposefully pick the large center booth that sits about six people. I like to call it

WHAT ARE YOU SENSING, SEEING, FEELING, OR HEARING FROM HIM?

_____

_____

_____

_____

_____

_____

_____

_____

_____

_____

_____

_____

_____

_____

our "prayer booth!" Those who know us visit our booth just to receive a prophetic word and prayer. We have been doing this for a couple years and it is so funny to watch them bring their friends to the jam *and* to our booth.

We had guests in our home and decided we'd invite them on a treasure hunt to our booth at the jam. Before leaving the house we ask God for "clues" to look out for. We each wrote down what God showed and put the words together like a puzzle. In this visit, we were to look out for someone with a hat, diamond earring, long hair and a blue shirt. The first person who walked up to our booth was a man. He had two of our clues; a hat and blue shirt. We told him he was our treasure and ask if he had pain in his body. He had pain in his shoulder and couldn't lift his arm up over his head. We all prayed for him and gave him a encouraging prophetic words then ask him to try to move his arm over his head. He lifted his arm up over his head and rubbed his shoulder surprised the pain was gone! He left and brought back a friend who had a sore hand. We prayed for the friend and his hand was healed.

Throughout the night we found about 10 people who had all or some of our clues. On the way out

WHAT ARE YOU SENSING, SEEING, FEELING, OR HEARING FROM HIM?

_____

_____

_____

_____

_____

_____

_____

_____

_____

_____

_____

_____

_____

_____

_____

the door, one of our guests saw a man across the room with a diamond earring. She was sure he was one of our treasures. It was late and he was busy talking to another group of musicians. I don't know how, but from across the crowded room he saw us start to leave and bolted through the crowd to ask us what we wanted to say to him! He was a Christian who needed prayer for marriage problems and felt the Lord tell him to catch up with us before we left!

Bethel's revivalists head to the streets looking for God's treasures. Teams head to the bars on Friday night bringing life and hope and come back with testimonies of healing, deliverance and salvation.

When I was in school of ministry we did outreach on Thursday afternoons. Our list of clues directed us to our community college. It was late in the day and not many people were still on campus. All of a sudden my friend saw someone off in the distance walking toward his car. She took off running after him, yelling, "Hey, wait…I want to talk to you." We took off running after her! I will never forget the look on his face. This beautiful girl with long blonde hair running like a gazelle in his direction wanting to talk with him! He stopped dead in his tracks! Although he may have thought she was flirting with him, her

WHAT ARE YOU SENSING, SEEING, FEELING, OR HEARING FROM HIM?

_____

_____

_____

_____

_____

_____

_____

_____

_____

_____

_____

_____

_____

_____

motive was to give him the encouraging word from the Lord.

We stayed back and let her talk with him and watched him wipe his eyes and look down toward his feet. Her word was about how God was going to bless his music and bring restoration in his family, especially with his dad. Come to find out his major was music and had never had a good relationship with his dad. The word from Heaven opened the door to pray for him and he received the Lord that day.

Again on a Thursday afternoon, we were led to horse stables near the river trail to heal someone with a back problem. We found our candidate right away and she was open for us to pray for her and her back was healed. We asked if there was anyone else we might be able to pray for and she told us one of the horses had a bad leg. So we headed into the stable and prayed for the horse's leg. She invited us outside to pray for her granddaughter who had restricted breathing and a lung disorder. Our team lay hands on her back and prayed and her breathing was easier.

Everyone was pretty excited about what was happening. One of the team noticed a horse on lead was limping. After praying for the horse, the owner continued walking the horse and the limp was gone!

WHAT ARE YOU SENSING, SEEING, FEELING, OR HEARING FROM HIM?

_____

_____

_____

_____

_____

_____

_____

_____

_____

_____

_____

_____

_____

_____

Driving back to the church we went over our testimony. A lady, a child, and two horses were healed! It was a good day!

The world is ripe for an encounter with Him and many Christians are strapped with stiff mindsets and religious form, unknowingly building barriers to the world. In John 4:35 we are told to "Open your eyes and look at the fields! They are ripe for harvest."

When we give people an encounter with Jesus, evangelism is easy.

Ask Papa God how you can build a prophetic outreach team to reach outside church walls. What would that look like in your community? Write out at least three ideas.

1._____

_____

_____

_____

2._____

_____

_____

_____

WHAT ARE YOU SENSING, SEEING, FEELING, OR HEARING FROM HIM?

_____

_____

_____

_____

_____

_____

_____

_____

_____

_____

_____

_____

_____

_____

_____

3._____

_____

_____

_____

_____

WHAT ARE YOU SENSING, SEEING, FEELING, OR HEARING FROM HIM?

_____

_____

_____

_____

_____

_____

_____

_____

_____

_____

_____

_____

_____

CHAPTER 7

GATES OF
PROPHETIC TESTIMONY

Jesus is our model. His relationship to the Father, His lifestyle of love as well as signs, wonders, and miracles are examples for us to follow. They are the testimony of Jesus. A testimony is proof, evidence, witness and demonstration, authentication, acknowledgment and declaration, an affidavit, deposition and record. Revelation 19:10 tells us the *"testimony of Jesus is the spirit of prophecy."*

WHAT ARE YOU SENSING, SEEING, FEELING, OR HEARING FROM HIM?

_____

_____

_____

_____

_____

_____

_____

_____

_____

_____

_____

_____

_____

_____

We, like Jesus, are destined to reveal our Papa God to the world by bearing His image. While all things are possible if we believe (Mark 9:23) all things are impossible without Him. Jesus was in communion with the Holy Spirit. That relationship teaches us what a Holy Spirit relationship looks like. It keeps us aware of God and His purpose rather than focusing on what we can do in our own strength. God raises up followers and friends, not leaders and servants. However, friends who follow Him make the most effective leaders who serve.

The testimonies of Jesus are our inheritance. Testimonies train us to fulfill our destiny as sons and daughters in the Kingdom. The power of testimony is seen through our own personal salvation experience. It is a first person encounter with the living God. Your personal testimony is the most powerful evangelistic tool you possess. When we share our testimony about receiving Christ or about His goodness, it draws others to Him.

My husband I weren't raised in Christian homes and both have experienced pain and trauma. God has healed us both and for 30 years we share the testimony of continued victory.

In one year, my husband and I recounted we had personally led over 2,000 people to Christ through sharing our personal testimonies and giving people an encounter with His presence.

WHAT ARE YOU SENSING, SEEING, FEELING, OR HEARING FROM HIM?

_____

_____

_____

_____

_____

_____

_____

_____

_____

_____

_____

_____

_____

_____

My testimony is even more powerful today then when I was first saved in 1978. I have written several books and magazine articles which included my testimony. My most recent book is entitled Dancing on the Graves of Your Past and has an accompanying workbook. My testimony has helped thousands of people find hope and healing. The strength of the victory and mercy of God is increased with each passing year.

Your personal testimony is the most powerful evangelistic tool you possess. Personal God encounters give you an anointing to see those same healing experiences manifest in others. Testimonies reveal God's nature and how He moves supernaturally. The nature of a testimony is that it draws attention to the reality of duplication. Testimonies increase faith in His ability to "do it again."

Write out your personal testimony of salvation, healing or the goodness of the Lord.

_____

_____

_____

_____

_____

_____

_____

_____

WHAT ARE YOU SENSING, SEEING, FEELING, OR HEARING FROM HIM?

_____

_____

_____

_____

_____

_____

_____

_____

_____

_____

_____

_____

_____

Years ago before I really had much exposure to healing ministry, we were in a meeting with someone who called people with bad backs or pelvic displacement to come forward for healing prayer. Soon the whole front row of chairs were filled with people needing healing. One of the symptoms of a bad back or misaligned pelvic is one leg would be shorter than the other. So he started lifting their legs to pray for the short leg to grow out and sure enough, the short legs grew out and backs were healed!

There were many people to pray for so he called me up to help. Well, I had a quick panic attack and stood silent because I had never seen legs grow out before, much less be the one who prayed! But it was the best experience I could have had. The first time He stood with me and showed me what to do and the person was healed. The next person I prayed for was healed, too. Every person in the meeting I prayed for with a bad back and one leg shorter than the other was healed! My faith to pray for short legs and bad backs was sky high!

Since that time, of course, my faith has grown to believe God for any need to be healed but it started with one person who believed in me. How much more does Jesus believe in us? He shows us what to do and invites us to follow His lead. The testimony of one person is contagious. Every opportunity is taken in our church to share testimonies of healing especially before praying for the sick.

What are you sensing, seeing, feeling, or hearing from Him?

_____

_____

_____

_____

_____

_____

_____

_____

_____

_____

_____

_____

_____

Jesus reveals himself through Divine encounters. The testimony of Jesus shifts the atmosphere into alignment with His power to save, heal and deliver.

Human resource statistics herald the epidemic rise in divorce, crime, drug dependence, disease, as well as overall emotional and economic decline. These alerts call the Christian to attention as they substantiate God's intention and desire to arrest the failing human spirit and bring life. Releasing God's love through the prophetic gives people an encounter with His love, presence and power. The prophetic releases "good news" from God and answers people's desperation for solution and resolve to their personal crises.

Record at least 5 testimonies you could share with someone.

1._____
_____
_____

2._____
_____
_____

WHAT ARE YOU SENSING, SEEING, FEELING, OR HEARING FROM HIM?

_____

_____

_____

_____

_____

_____

_____

_____

_____

_____

_____

_____

_____

_____

3._____

_____

_____

4._____

_____

_____

5._____

_____

_____

WHAT ARE YOU SENSING, SEEING, FEELING, OR HEARING FROM HIM?

_____

_____

_____

_____

_____

_____

_____

_____

_____

_____

_____

_____

_____

_____

Impartation

Place your hand on your stomach and pray with me. As you pray do a prophetic act and step out of any box of constraint and receive His anointing.

Papa God,
I release greater third Heaven encounters,
revelation and understanding,
wisdom and greatness.
I release confidence in anointing and gifting,
courage and faith.
I arise up to Your calling and commissioning.
I sit in my seat in Heavenly places with You!
Papa, I say 'yes'
let's go change the world!

ABOUT THE AUTHOR
YVONNE MARTINEZ

With 25 years experience in prophetic pastoring, emotional healing and trauma resolution, Yvonne serves on Pastoral Counseling staff in the Transformation Center at Bethel Church in Redding, CA.

Yvonne is an author, conference speaker, third-year Bethel School of Supernatural Ministry graduate, and hosts articles and Q/A column for the Christian Quarterly entitled Talk With Yvonne.

As an ordained minister, Yvonne's passion is to see people acquire their Kingdom identity, inheritance, intimacy and authority. She is available for speaking or personal ministry.

OTHER BOOKS:

Dancing on the Graves of Your Past
(book and workbook)

Prayers of Prophetic Declaration

Angel Feathers – Chronicle Heavenly Adventures

CONTACT

Yvonne Martinez

(530) 255-2099 x 1921

yvonnem@ibethel.org

or

talkwithyvonne@hotmail.com

Books available at

www.StillwaterLavender.com

14695707R00088

Made in the USA
San Bernardino, CA
03 September 2014